C is for CEO

A Kid's Introduction to Business

Written by Aaron White
Illustrated by Sam Jacobs
Edited by Kelsey White

ISBN 979-8-218-26081-1

Written by Aaron White
Illustrated by Sam Jacobs
Cover Design by Sam Jacobs
Edited by Kelsey White
Layout by Elizabeth Hunt

From the Author:

This book is made to **create conversations** around goals and success. What does success look like for your family? What does it mean to always try hard? This book is made to help children understand that anything is possible (no matter what they decide to do), while introducing some new concepts around entrepreneurship, startups, and what it takes to create and reach their dreams.

– Aaron White

A

is for ambition–
remember to always try hard.

B is for business—
let's make your first card!

C is for CEO –
they shoot for the stars!

D is for determination—
it will get you to Mars!

E is for effort–

it's when you try your best.

F is for finance—
spend some, invest the rest.

G

is for Golden Rule—
let's use it as our guide.

H is for hiring—
you'll need great people
by your side.

I is for investor—
they want to see it pay.

J is for job—
it's where you'll work each day.

K is for keynote—
it's when you share your plan.

L is for liquidity–
it's all about cash in hand.

M is for market—
we need to find our fit.

N is for NDA—
don't blab, even a bit!

O is for opportunity-

take everyone you find.

P is for product—
keep your customers in mind.

Q is for qualified—
because that's what you are.

R is for revenue—
it's how we got so far.

S is for small talk—
it gets easier, we swear.

T is for taxes—
it's how we pay our share.

U is for understanding–
always make sure you listen.

V is for venture capital—
they would love to support your vision.

W is for win–

celebrate them big and small.

X is for exit—
it's when you pass the ball.

Y is for yearly goals—

improving yourself is smart.

What goals do you have this year?

Z is for zero—
because that is where we start.

But with effort, friends,
and help, we will see...

the great success we all
know you'll be!